Foster Care: Not Broken, Just Bent

JESSICA ROSE CASTILLO

~CONTENTS~

ACKNOWLEDGEMENTS

"The following people helped me get to where I am today in ways you couldn't begin to imagine. They have encouraged me to follow my dreams and be the best that I can, and for this I will be forever grateful."

-Jessica Rose Castillo

Amanda Canfield
Christopher Canfield
Addison Cooper
Suzy Millar

I would also like to thank the staff and teachers at **William S. Hart High School** for your constant encouragement, understanding, and patience throughout the duration of my enrollment. You have made one of the most difficult parts of my life also one of the most enjoyable, and memorable. A special thank you to **Ray Archer** and **Hart Show Choir** for teaching me things that went beyond the textbook and into my everyday life. Thank you **Rooted Youth Group** for providing me with the balance I needed to succeed as a teenager, thank you **Chelsea O'neale** for providing me with the most genuine care a social worker has to offer, and thank you to my mother - you have loved me

through your toughest moments and mine as well,
and that is all I could ever ask of you.

INTRODUCTION

I would like to start off our journey together through your reading of "Foster Care - Not Broken, Just Bent" by saying thank you. Thank you for supporting my desire to educate and inspire by reading what insight I have to offer you, and most of all, thank you for deciding to embark on one of the most rewarding experiences you could ever hope to be a part of - dedicating your life to becoming a foster or adoptive parent. It takes a special kind of person to be willing to put in the time, energy, and dedication it takes to fulfill this role.

Speaking of time, energy, and dedication… it takes a *lot* of it! I'm here to give you what I believe to be some of the most crucial information in foster parenting - well, crucial from the viewpoint of a former foster child, I suppose. From as far back as I can remember until the age of 11, I lived in a terribly abusive environment. From 11 to 16, I was a foster child. From 16 to 17, I was adopted. From 17 to now, well, I'm working on the aftermath of the last 20-something years! On my journey to healing, I get the exceptionally joyful (cue sarcasm) opportunity to remember things that have hurt me and that have helped sculpt me into the person I am today. Yes, there are countless memories I have that, on a good day, outweigh all the negative ones by a landslide. Though, I would be lying if I said there weren't any memories that keep me in bed for a couple of days; memories primarily (though not exclusively) from the moment I was taken away to the moment I turned 18.

There are foster parents, social workers, etc. who give the system a terrible image, and I want to help fix that by remembering what made my experience so painful and using that to make sure it doesn't happen to any other child. This change needs to happen ... and it starts with you and the knowledge and tips you are given going into this. In reading *"Foster Care - Not Broken, Just Bent"*, I will explain everything from home life to school, to behaviors, backgrounds, and how to properly handle all of it - all from the perspective of someone who spent the most confusing and vulnerable years in a person's life (we all know this one - tweens/teens) experiencing all that makes the foster care system a scary place.

CHAPTER ONE: FOSTER CARE, NOT *CARELESS*

The Many Definitions of "Foster Care"

If you were to google search "define foster care", the first definition you will see is the following from *Wikipedia*:

> "**Foster Care** is a system in which a minor has been placed into a ward, group home, or private home of a state-certified caregiver, referred to as a '**Foster Parent**'"

Merriam-Webster defines foster care as "*a situation in which for a period of time a child lives with and is <u>cared for</u> by people who are not the child's parents.*" The *International Foster Care Organization* (IFCO) defines foster care as "*a way of providing a family life for children who cannot live with their own parents.*" One definition that many former foster children can relate to is from the *Urban Dictionary*, stating that foster care is "*a way of punishing children through the ages of infants to 18 (and sometimes older) for what their parents did*". That last one got *real*.

Reading through those few definitions of the system, I would like to point out that out of the three that are not decorated by popular opinion (referring to the *Urban Dictionary's* definition), only one of them uses the word "care" in describing the responsibilities of the foster care system. That disturbs me deeply, because not everybody knows how to read into the other definitions and gather that in providing for, caring for, and taking care *of* a child, it goes far deeper than simply providing clothes, food and shelter (all of which are equally important, don't get me wrong). For example, when I moved into my third foster home, I was absolutely devastated. I had - for the most part - enjoyed my second foster home, the friends I had, my school, etc. When my third foster mom, Emma, opened the door and saw me crying, the first thing she told me was - and I will never forget this - "stop that crying right now or I'll send you to a group home, you cannot cry in this house". In addition to total lack of empathy and consideration towards her foster children's feelings, at the start of each child's stay in her home she would buy you three pairs of underwear from the .99 cent store, a pair of khaki pants and a collared shirt from Goodwill, then say "you go to a school with uniforms, you have no need for any other clothes. That's your parents' problem, not mine". She had the same philosophy about food, too. Since we got lunch at school, she saw no need for us to eat that often at the house. Every once in a while she would cook a nice meal, but on most occasions if we were hungry at home we either snuck peanut butter jars up the stairs or were sat down at the table and forced to eat all the food that was expired.

In the eyes of Emma, being a foster parent was merely a job that made it possible for her to buy big TV's and an RV. In my eyes at the time, my definition would have been no different than the *Urban Dictionary's.* Right now, I see what it was supposed to be, what it is, and what it could be. What will it be? A lot of it is up to you as a foster parent, and how you decide to make it.

Jessica's definition of Foster Care:

> Foster Care is when a child has not had the easiest life, thus they are removed from the home and the situations that they know and are placed into homes and situations that *should* be safer and make it possible for the child to grow as a person. A foster home should provide love, care both physically and emotionally, and support - and not just for the money.

You will be what defines the foster care system for those that you care for, make sure it isn't similar to the *Urban Dictionary's.*

There are plenty of hopes a person could have when deciding to become a foster parent. Some are positive and very bright-eyed, such as wanting to be able to share your "picket fence, fireplace, pies cooling on the windowsill" home-life fantasy with children who are less fortunate. Others are far more selfish, hoping that in becoming a foster parent they will gain a lot of money, bragging rights (such as at your church or in your community, for example), and not actually have to *care* about any of the children - basically hoping it will be easy money.

The reality of becoming a foster parent is the same as becoming a parent in general - it is not all about you anymore, you are *caring* for a child, and how you decide to care for that child will help define who they will become when they are older. In addition - it is not easy money. The money you receive is for the child you are caring for, not for your brand new purse or swimming pool.

Becoming a foster parent is not to help you achieve a life of luxury, but to provide a life worth living for someone who has not had that. This is why it takes a very special kind of person to become a foster parent; you must be selfless, a quality too many people lack these days.

What is a **selfish intention**? You would think this would be an easy question to answer, especially after the examples given above. Though, not everyone would think that even the "pie in the windowsill" fantasy might be selfish as well. You have an idea of what you want your foster family to look like, and that in and of itself will bring you disappointment and frustration. Why is this? You will have children from all different walks of life, some having experienced abuse far beyond your fathomability. To try to have so many different types of people conform to one common way of living will not work with foster children, and could even be terrifying to some - which is an unfair situation to expect or even hope for a child to adapt to so quickly.

 To give you an example of this, my first foster home was terribly unaccepting of me and my inability to quickly adapt to their home and lifestyle. It was an all hispanic household, and unfortunately my father was a racist man and had imprinted into my young brain an awful image of how hispanic families functioned (though I never agreed, I had gone to a very diverse elementary school and enjoyed my classmates), thus making the first night at my first foster home absolutely terrifying for me. They didn't expect for a little girl to be sensitive to their foods, to not understand what they were saying, or to be intimidated by their *ethnicity* due to her father's terrible ideals. The foster mother would get angry at me for not being able to keep down her cooking (we couldn't afford a lot of healthy foods growing up, so once I was taken away it took my body a while to adapt to eating a variety of legitimate foods), and began threatening me with the P.E.T. team (psychiatric emergency team) every time I was too scared to eat her food. She would get angry with me on a daily basis, for little things I didn't know how to control (such as my inability to understand the spanish language, my tummy's reactions to her foods, and my panic attacks), and this made me increasingly nervous. Not a day went by when I didn't cry myself to sleep, or wake up nervous as to how the day was going to pan out. I could not get myself to stop thinking "how is this situation better than the one that I knew how to deal with? One with a loving mother?"; every new day fueled my overwhelming sadness and depression.

Imagine you just moved to a new school in the middle of the school year, and everyone expected you to instantly understand what was going on and to be able to go about every day as if you had always been there. Can you just imagine how scary that would be? Even if you were given a quick summary of how things functioned and what the class had already learned, it would still be extremely intimidating and anxiety-provoking. Or you can remember back to when you were very young, and your mom had to come pick you up in the middle of the night from the sleepover at your friend's house because you were too afraid to be away from home. Multiply either of those by maybe 10, and you may have a general understanding of how scary it is to move into your new foster home, and how scarier it is to be expected to adjust to it all right away.

The reality is that it is not easy; not for you or the child, at least not in the beginning. With the right amount of time and patience, it will only get easier, and more beautiful - just like any other blossoming relationship. You just can't rush it.

CHAPTER TWO - WHO, WHAT, AND WHY

Backgrounds and Lifestyles

I remember my third foster home vividly. We constantly had girls coming and going, and normally had more girls in the home than what was legally allowed. I remember on two occasions when my foster sisters were told over the phone by their biological mothers that "they should have had an abortion", which made me sad for them because I have always been very close to my mom. There were also girls who had suffered extreme sexual abuse, who had drug addictions, who were lesbians, who had abortions, who had lost their parents completely, and those who adored their parents and counted down the days until each visit. Thus being said, you will have many different children placed in your home. Different in age, gender, and background.

Because of the wide variety of characters you will come into contact with, you must greet each child individually and openly, doing your very best to have no preconceived judgments or immediate expectations. You will know what you have read and what you have heard, but you have not yet experienced living with this child yourself. Take time to get to know them - their likes, dislikes, favorite animals, etc.

Start off with surface level subjects such as school, animals, games, things that take away from the severity of the current situation and that distract the child from the past and encourage them to focus on the present and what is good about it.

While doing so, however, remember not to push it. If the child does not have much to say, don't try to drag information out of them. Simply try to find a subject they seem most comfortable talking about and pursue *that.* Even spending some of that time that they are silent by talking about yourself would be a good idea, so they feel like you're less of a stranger and more of a friend (or friend to be), and that you care about them knowing about you just as much as you want to know about them... which I believe shows that you genuinely want to develop a relationship. Spend the first few days with this child getting to know them and internalizing what seems to make them comfortable and uncomfortable.

Previous lifestyles must be considered as well. One child may have fallen asleep with the television on and with commotion, whereas another may have slept in pure silence and darkness. One child watched TV all day while drawing pictures, and another child might have played outside until dinnertime. I would say that it is a good idea to allow the child entering your home to be able to integrate some of the harmless everyday activities that they're used to into this new home life they must learn to live, in order to help them adjust to the newness of the whole situation slowly and with ease, and with the least amount of anxiety. Eventually they will be more willing to compromise, once they feel more comfortable.

In most of my foster homes, I only had to live with teenage girls. Never co-ed, and only once with younger children (two, about elementary school age). More likely than not, the teenagers you welcome into your home have not had much of a childhood, and have had to grow up very young. On the other hand, the younger children you are bringing in still have the opportunity to enjoy being, well, a *child.*

It's difficult for children of all ages, but in different ways. I remember two girls - sisters - who I had lived with, one was 17 and the other was 9. The older sister had experienced terrible abuse, remembered it all, and remembered her sister being abused as well. Her sister, being so young, did not remember much about the abuse in their home (they had both been in foster care for a good handful of years at this point). It put a strain on the sisters and their hopes, goals, expectations, etc. The oldest sister was very concerned with the wellbeing of her younger sister, but did not take much time to focus on herself and what she was going to do once she aged out of the system; she was too busy being a mother to her motherless sister. Obviously, this shouldn't have been her role to fill. She was still - though most teenagers don't like to accept this - a kid, who was about to become an adult. Today, she has two young children that she had right after highschool - and directly following her aging out of the foster care system - , and she is working very hard on herself and her family. What makes me sad when I think about it, is that she never really got to enjoy any part of her childhood, she always had to be the "adult". Whereas I know it's important to prepare teenagers for adulthood, to treat them very seriously and teach them the importance of responsibility and accountability, etc. I find them being able to *finally* enjoy not having to worry, not having to be the adult in their homes, equally important.

You not only have the opportunity to provide a better childhood for children who are young, but for teenagers as well; you have the power to make their final years before adulthood enjoyable, memorable, and impactful.

Something I also believe to be of great importance on the topic of age is to realize that some of these children may have not been taught what you feel to be common sense or necessary habits to have at their age, such as general manners, or for the older ones things like doing laundry, or even the ever-so-popular "respect your elders". Be aware of the healthy and the unhealthy habits the youth tend to portray, and address them with gentility and sensitive correction rather than judgement. You don't want them to take anything too personally, taking your corrections or suggestions as personal attacks rather than necessary lessons, or even feel that you are attacking their parents' way of raising them (this may not be a problem for all children, but I know for me, I was always ready to jump at the chance to defend my mother and the way she brought me up, regardless of whether it was right or wrong).

It is also important to realize when a habit needs addressing and when it doesn't. If the specific habit the child portrays is wrong, unhealthy, dangerous, etc. then clearly it is appropriate to address the habit and help the child develop healthier ways of living. Though, if you simply find something the child does to be odd or different, such as their bedtime routines or how they put on their shoes for example, it does not necessarily mean they are doing it incorrectly. I would say in a situation like this, show interest in the child's habit, not questioning them in a way that portrays concern, disgust, or even in a manner that deems condescending or belittling, but more as a way of getting to know them in order to avoid the child feeling threatened, because again - it could be taken very personally, very quickly. At this point, once you realize the child's reasoning behind their habits, you can then decide if it is *necessary* to teach the child differently.

In regards to teenagers specifically, they tend to already have established their own way of thinking, talking, acting, etc. So, in these situations, it is crucial to not come from a point of judgment, but more curiosity and interest. Coming off as condescending to a teenager can backfire *very* quickly, and make the general home environment not very comfortable. If you see something they do as unhealthy, or unnecessary, I feel that addressing it in a way that has more of a "hey, did you know?" kind of approach rather than a "that's not the way it should be done" standpoint, you will be a lot more successful.

Sort of remaining on the topic of lifestyles, backgrounds, and even age - it's important for *your* feelings to know that a lot of foster children's initial reactions to people, situations, or things that you say and do, are not meant to be personal attacks. Most of the time, they are all on "defense mode". Having been hurt so terribly by the people they trusted so wholey, it makes sense that a child would have their guard up and be terribly hesitant to let it down. Thus being said, there will be situations that will sting.

For example, you might make efforts to become close to them, and they could shut that down quickly. Ouch! The primary reasoning behind this is simply that they do not want to be hurt again, and rightfully so. A big reason for many children is also that they don't want to replace their parents, and they feel that you might be trying to take on that role in their lives that they don't want filled by anyone else. I would say, in trying to make efforts such as these, always be aware of how you are presenting yourself. If you are trusted first as a friend, you will soon be trusted as - dare I say - a parental figure.

You will find this in foster children of all ages. Just know that the responses they have to you are not all meant to be taken personally, but are merely a form of defense and their feeling that they need to protect themselves, and sometimes even their parents. More often than not the first reaction will always be as if they are being attacked, but over time as they get to know you and develop a trusting relationship with you, I guarantee that this will not be as big of a problem.

Take most negative reactions to your innocent intentions with a grain of salt, but also try to assess why they may have had such a negative reaction in the first place and what you think could be done differently in the future to help avoid that. Foster parenting takes a lot of continuous assessment and thinking, doesn't it? You will see just how worth it all ends up being in due time, though. I promise.

CHAPTER THREE - LOVE LANGUAGES AND COMMUNICATION

The Levels of Love and When it's Enough

We all love people differently, and portray that love differently as well. One person could love their mother by sending her flowers every week and having lunch every Sunday, and someone else could show love to their mother simply by trying to do well in their own lives, to show their mom that she did good and should be proud. There are countless ways for a person to show love to a friend, family member, lover, etc., and this is crucial to keep in mind when fostering a child.

To cover the basics, here are the five languages of love according to Dr. Gary Chapman:
1. <u>WORDS OF AFFIRMATION</u> - This is when one's love language is centered around words both said and heard. A compliment can go a long way, while an insult or words spoken in a negative manner will cut deep. Saying "I love you" or the lack thereof will have more extreme reactions as well.
2. <u>QUALITY TIME</u> - This particular language requires that one receives another person's undivided attention in order to feel loved, and vice versa in showing it. Being ignored,

barely paid attention to, or even having their plans changed by you could greatly impact their ideas of how you feel about them. Be there for them, that's the most important thing you could do.

3. <u>RECEIVING GIFTS</u> - For some, receiving occasional, meaningful gifts is what makes them feel the most loved, valued, and appreciated.

4. <u>ACTS OF SERVICE</u> - Lending a helping hand, keeping promises, favors, all of these things show you value them and your relationship with them. If you are not a "man of your word" or are not willing to help them out when they need it, they will feel as if they hold no real significance in your life and that they are not worth your time.

5. <u>PHYSICAL TOUCH</u> - Hugs, hand shakes, everything that *appropriately* shows your genuine care for this person will mean more than anything else you could do for them. For example, my mom was always hugging me, rubbing my back or touching my shoulder, it made me feel valued. There are times when I feel if a friend or family member does not want to touch me, that they are not comfortable with me and therefore do not truly love me, so I relate most to this form of love language! Just try not to seem too distant.

Of course, just because a person prefers one out of these five more than the others, it does not mean you shouldn't practice a little bit of them all.

The thing about foster children and their love languages of choice is that they may be more hesitant in receiving *any* form of love from you for a good amount of time in the beginning, and this is something that should not be taken personally. You should follow the child's pace, but at the same time do not leave it all up to them - doing this might come off as you being completely disinterested in them rather than simply respecting their current boundaries. Give a little, get a little, and so on.

Try to be aware of what they respond most positively to, and then go from there, and remember...there is a difference between being *different* and *indifferent*. Don't *ever* forget that.

Sticks and stones can break my bones, but words will never hurt me.

My mom used to tell me this all the time when I was in elementary school, but no matter how hard I tried, it always seemed to be the opposite for me. I could be hit, punched, slapped, or I could trip and fall, and of course it would hurt. Though, in time, those wounds healed and were easily forgotten. When someone says something mean, hurtful, downright terrible.. it doesn't just hurt, but it scars. I remember not only the terrible things my father said to *me* when I was younger, but my *mother* as well. Both equally as painful and nearly impossible to forget. Words stick, wounds heal.

It is important to be mindful of what you say and how you say it to foster youth. In addition, know that it could be equally if not *more* hurtful for you to say something negative or insulting about their parents. I remember back in foster care if someone said something mean to me, I would just swallow it and hurt later on when I was alone. Though, what *really* hurt me - deep to the core - was when they would say something hurtful about my mother, even in a joking manner. It would just rip me apart. All social workers and foster parents see is what's on the surface, but believe it or not - there are some foster children who might have had good relationships with some of their family or one of their parents, maybe even both parents. So, to bash the child's parents in any way shape or form, even passively, it could hurt them in such a way that creates a permanent wall between you and the child. If you hope to have any relationship with the child, or trust from them, I would avoid speaking ill of their family, especially their parents.

A quick trip down the path of quantum physics will reveal to you that the deliberate choices we make create the realities we desire, and words are an extremely significant tool we use in this process. The words we say and words we receive affect our personal "energies", the vibrations that make us feel and make us who we are, the vibrations that ultimately make up our thought processes and how we react to the world.

I have read an article recently that had discussed a fascinating experiment done by the Japanese scientist *Masaru Emoto* in the 1990's regarding the effect words have on energy. In this experiment, he pointed out that water free from all impurities will create enchanting ice crystals when frozen, only increasing in beauty when inspected closely underneath a microscope. If water has been polluted and is flooded with impurities, it will not freeze in a way that creates such beautiful formations. Emoto had poured pure water into two separate containers, labeling them with negative phrases such as "fear" and "I hate you", etc. This resulted in the water being grey and clumpy rather than gracefully elegant snowflakes. Emoto's next step was to place positive phrases such as "I love you" and "peace" on to vials that contained heavily polluted water, and after just 24 hours they produced perfectly hexagonal crystals. These experiments proved that positive and negative words have a great impact on energy, enough so that it can actually change the physical structure of an object. The fascinating results of his experiments have been detailed in a series of books such as **The Hidden Messages in Water** (this being the first of the series). In these books you can actually see the results of these experiments, which is astounding to say the least.

Aside from the "zen water experiments" and "quantum physics", we have been taught from many different sources that "if you don't have anything nice to say, don't say anything at all" - the golden rule. Being a foster parent is about promoting a healthy, enjoyable life for a child who has not had that chance, giving them the opportunity to grow and develop the confidence they need to succeed in life and overall love themselves. There is not a truly positive outcome for negativity in any situation, and there is a difference between being stern, parental, and responsible and being mean, condescending, and negative. Teach children through kindness, especially those who have been hurt. Thus being said, if you don't have anything nice to say...don't say anything at all.

Punishments and Consequences

Sticks and stones, the golden rule, of course those are important concepts to keep in mind when parenting a child who has experienced trauma. However, you are then faced with situations that actually do require a more negative response. By a negative response, I mean this; a child lies, a child breaks something, a child hurts another child, etc. These are all negative actions, and of course must be dealt with in a way that teaches the child right from wrong. Positive actions receive positive consequences, and unfortunately negative actions receive negative consequences - that's just life, and don't we all know it! Therefore, children who do wrong, suffer the consequences.

Consequences are crucial in developing a child's sense of right and wrong, good and bad, etc. However, the unfortunate reality is that punishments and consequences can be taken very personally, and very differently than intended if not properly explained to a child who has been through a lot. Even the anticipation of punishments/consequences could be enough to terrify a child, depending on how their parents had handled similar situations in the past. Who knows, maybe they've never even received any consequences for their actions!

Possibly the best way to approach a foster child who has done wrong, is to incorporate constant reassurance, so that they do not question even for a moment whether or not they are still loved, or important. At the same time, ensuring that the child is internalizing the fact that lessons need to be learned in order for them to get the best things out of life, and stay out of trouble and negative situations that can be avoided. Communication is key; as long as they fully understand the severity of their wrongdoing and why it is that they must experience a negative consequence to go with their actions, then I feel that the situation has been handled well and the child will grow from the experience.

Another important rule to live by; "Do unto others as you would have them do unto you". They've got to understand that just as much as they don't like being treated in negative ways, others don't feel any better about it either. Just remember to approach the situation sternly, yet from a place of love...and this must be made clear to the child. Constant reassurance may not seem so important in your mind, but I can guarantee that it will have the most positive results on your foster child.

More often than not, the child has experienced situations in which negativity was rewarded, or right and wrong had different meanings, or where situations were handled in such a way that caused hurt onto someone. So, when punishing a foster child, do your best to understand their reasonings before jumping to punish, because they may think they're in the right. It's your job to tell them that what they think is right, might not actually be right.

CHAPTER FOUR - HOME LIFE

The Fruits of the Spirit

Whether you consider yourself to be religious, spiritual, or neither, the fruits of the spirit are all characteristics that will only bring positivity to yourself, your surroundings, and those you surround yourself with. In strengthening these attributes, you will find it to be most beneficial in dealing with situations you are not familiar with, situations that frustrate or confuse you, and overall - most situations you will find yourself in as a foster parent!

So what are the fruits of the spirit?

- LOVE
- JOY
- PEACE
- PATIENCE
- GOODNESS
- KINDNESS
- GENTLENESS
- SELF CONTROL
- FAITHFULNESS

The fruits of the spirit are important characteristics to have in order to enjoy your life to its fullest and get the most out of it, though there are situations that call for each of them more than the other in order to ensure consistent comfortability in your life and genuine happiness. Now, I would like to discuss how I feel these "fruits" will best help you foster in such a way that creates a consistently comfortable, enjoyable life for both you and the children.

- **LOVE**

  Love is something that should be incorporated into everything that you do - your language towards the child, your actions and intentions, and the overall environment and energy of your home. All that you do should be done out of love, and **in the best interest of the child.**

- **JOY**

  As you well know, and as previously discussed, the vast majority of foster children have not had the luxury of being able to enjoy their childhood. From trips to the park, to surprise ice cream trips after school, even to a simple Disney movie night where everyone gets to pick a snack from the market and watch a movie in the living room. Not only will doing things that are joyful for the whole family be a good way to bond with the children and create delightful memories, but it will improve the overall atmosphere of your everyday life, and the children will increasingly enjoy their home lives rather than resenting them for one reason or another. A foster home shouldn't feel like a jail, but a *home.* Individual time with each child is crucial as well - creating joyful moments with each child both individually *and* together as a unit will only improve the overall functionality of the home and the respect, trust, and love between its inhabitants.

- **PEACE**

Peace is arguably the most important factor to maintain in your home. Peace is a foreign concept to these children, having experienced little to none of it in their previous home lives. It is necessary to watch the tone that is used, the words that are said, the noise levels, the tension levels, etc. to ensure a comfortable living environment for everyone within the home. Situations that are flooded with negativity and anger could bring up terrible memories for the children that could stop them from being able to move forward in their lives and potentially make things tense for everyone in the home. Overall, you don't need to walk on eggshells… but you do need to be mindful of what the children's previous home lives might have been, and provide them with what they *should* have had all along - **Peace.**

- **PATIENCE**

Patience is crucial in ensuring a home life that functions smoothly and with ease, as well as promoting a healthy growing environment for the foster children in your home. In showing patience towards foster children, you are leading by example - you show patience to them, they show patience towards others, thus they flourish and make the most of all situations they are involved in. It teaches them to not think impulsively, unlike those they may have been surrounded by in their previous homes. It's one thing to be patient with adults, it's another to be patient with children, and it's a whole different thing to show patience to foster children. It can take away from the fear of doing something wrong and enable them to grow and learn through their mistakes rather than not take responsibility, which will create a much more trusting environment for everyone in the home. I read an article recently (I know, I read a lot of articles) that had suggested a few things in regards to parents showing patience to their children. One was to underreact to things, because in doing so it prevents you from getting caught up in the emotions of a situation and gives you the clarity you need to really look at a situation and figure out what the best solution would be. Another concept that was discussed was a child's reaction to **facial expressions**, which is certainly something I can relate to - your reactions, such as shock or

curiosity, may cause you to crinkle
your eyebrows or instinctively make
a face, and a child can see this and
interpret it as anger. A study done
has proven that the brains of most
kids that are around middle school
aged cannot completely make out
the meanings of most facial
expressions and often end up
assuming in the end. Doing your
best to react less with your face and
try to keep a "botox brow" (basically
just nothing too extreme) could
make the child feel safer in
approaching you with everything
from a problem to a confession of
bad behavior, which will only
strengthen your relationship and
your trust.

- **GOODNESS**

    Goodness is doing the right thing, for
    the right reason. This is a simple
    concept that is surprisingly difficult
    for most people to act out. It's much
    easier to either do the right thing for
    the wrong reason or the wrong thing
    for the right reason. For example, as

previously discussed, simply
becoming a foster parent for the
sake of money, or even self
righteousness is doing the right thing
for the wrong reasons. Think deeply
about the reality of your intentions.

- **KINDNESS**

*"No act of kindness, no matter how
small, is ever wasted."*

-

AESOP
*"Kindness is the language which the
deaf can hear and the blind can
see."*

-MARK

TWAIN
"Carry out a random act of kindness,
with no expectation of reward,
*safe in the knowledge that one day
someone might do the same for
you."*

-

PRINCESS DIANA

Aesop, Mark Twain, Princess Diana,
we've heard those with exceptional
wisdom and intelligence speak of

kindness as a necessity of life, a significant factor on the journey to pure and genuine happiness...though we all treat it like a characteristic only portrayed by those who are weak in nature. In the truest of realities, however, kindness is the image of strength that has nothing to hide - *true* strength.

Show kindness to your foster children, and they will show kindness to others. It's as simple and significant as that. Don't allow pride, greed, arrogance, ignorance, or anything of that nature to repress you from being able to not only encourage these children to live a life of genuinity and good humanity...but you as well. Only good things can come from kindness.

- **GENTLENESS**

In the dictionary, gentleness is described as being overall tender, and acting in a caring manner. *Gentleness* is quite possibly the most useful tool that allows us to undo the ways in which we have been conditioned to live, and showing tenderness towards foster children will teach them this as well, which is *crucial* in allowing them to live a life of their own, rather than continuing to live in the past and in what they have come to know. Even for those who have not had particularly difficult lives have been taught to be harsh, tough, desensitized to the nature of who we really are, which is far more delicate than we would like to admit. In practicing and encouraging gentility in our everyday lives, we are able to really evaluate the areas of our lives where we are exceptionally hard and rough, with not only ourselves but others, and in beginning to understand this we are able to change it for the better of our own well being and those around us.

- **SELF CONTROL**

It is terribly difficult for people of all ages to perform consistent acts of self control, from little things like sticking to exercise things to larger things such as acting out in a restaurant because your meal was not up to your standards. In regards to parenting, especially as a foster parent, it is terribly important that you maintain a constant state of self control when dealing with situations that involve the foster children. To set an example, to gain and maintain their trust, to show them that acting out in life is not the answer. My father was a man notorious for getting drunk and acting out, then having too much arrogance to accept responsibility for the outcomes of his actions and would then put it off on someone else - nothing was ever his fault. It gave me crippling anxiety starting at the young age of nine, and lack of self control of the adults in your living environment as a kid is scary, because you never know what they expect or how to react. Self control is important, because you don't want to put these children in similar situations to what they've been brought up on.

- **FAITHFULNESS**

  To be faithful is to be true to one's word, dependable, constant. Have faith in your foster children, in yourself, and don't break your foster children's faith in you… and watch everyone flourish.

  If a foster child has faith in you, please, do not betray that.

ROOMMATES

Throughout the duration of my time spent in the foster care system, I have had a minimum of 16 roommates that I can remember - all different races, ages, styles, backgrounds, different levels of brokenness, and so on. Growing up, I was always being bullied, both at school and at home, and unfortunately it didn't stop once I was taken away. I have two painfully vivid memories of being threatened to be "jumped" by my first foster sisters, and actually being beaten up by some of the girls from my third home. I'm very sensitive, I have a lot of emotions...and somehow I found myself always being placed in homes that were flooded with insensitive, downright cruel people - mean girls! Being older and not in the middle of those situations anymore, I now understand that most of what made the other girls mean was what made me fragile - just different reactions to different levels of trauma (though I still can't put my finger on why the foster parents were just as - if not more - mean). There are a handful of things I would like to cover in this section, but let's focus more on some basics that can prove to be very helpful when it comes to making roommate decisions.

Here are the top 5 factors to consider when deciding who will be roommates:

1. **AGE**

   This one's a little more obvious;
   teenagers with teenagers, children
   with children. Teenagers can talk
   about their feelings and troubles
   amongst each other, and children
   can talk about playing and school
   and such, and they can do this with
   ease because they feel they can
   relate more to one another because
   they're similar in age

2. **SIBLINGS**

   If you are presented with the
   opportunity to pair siblings together,
   do it. If there is at all a chance to
   keep siblings together, it should
   always be done. They're familiar
   with each other, comfortable with
   each other, and feel safe with each
   other, and to break that up could be
   devastating.

3. **PERSONALITIES**

   This one's a little difficult, because
   you do have to learn to live amongst
   people of all different
   personalities...but it's different when
   it comes to your home. Children
   should feel safe at home, *especially*

in their rooms. Pairing a child who has fits of anger with a child who has panic attacks and is painfully shy for example might create an extremely tense and stressful living environment for the children, ultimately making home life as a whole more difficult. Try to be as mindful as possible, doing your best to use the knowledge you have to pair similar personalities with each other to create a feeling of safety and joy in the home, rather than nervousness and tension, is extremely important.

4. QUIRKS

Growing up, there was not a night where the television wasn't on, most of the time alongside my mom doing dishes and the lights being on (I slept on the floor in the living room of our one bedroom apartment, so I was in the center of it all). When I was taken away, I had spent 11 years of my life only being able to fall asleep with the television on, and once that was taken away from me, I could only fall asleep by crying myself to sleep after having a panic attack, or if one of my foster sisters would sleep with me (which didn't sit well with my foster parents). Some children are afraid of the dark, some need to fall asleep to music or the television, some need to say prayers before bed, some need to maintain constant organization, others feel more at ease with some clutter, and so on. If you know some of the quirks the foster children have, do your very best to take them into consideration when setting up roommates, If you don't know any, ask! "Is there anything that would make you feel more at home? Do you have any special requests that would make things easier?" etc.

5. DURATION OF STAY

This one is a little difficult to consider when rooming foster children together, because most of the time you don't know exactly how long a child will be living with you. A good way to look at it, though, would be to use the knowledge you do have to room youth who are going to be in the system for a long time together, and youth who may be in the system for a shorter length of time together. I feel that this adds a sense of stability to the situation.

Having roommates won't always be rainbows and sunshine to some of the kids you will foster, but it will definitely have some joyful moments if even just a little bit of thought goes into how you set up the roommates, and could make all the difference in your foster child's everyday attitude.

Personal Items

This is a very, very serious subject that requires a lot of respect on your part as foster parents. As a foster child, you feel as if everything you've come to know and love has been ripped away from you in the blink of an eye, and that all you have left to hold onto and cherish are the few possessions you take with you as you move around. From pictures to toys, to ripped blankets or even a particular pair of socks...foster children can often attach memories or significant meaning onto these items, making them far more significant in the maintenance of the child's sanity and feeling of security than anyone could even try to understand. Losing a button, or finding a scratch or rip on something could have a reaction that to you may look at as awfully exaggerated and silly, but to the child it feels like the straw that broke the camel's back.

Another aspect in regards to a foster child's possessions is that aside from the fact that they may have attached irreplaceable worth to an item, subconsciously their personal items signify a far deeper meaning than simply being their "things" - those items they carry with them, *they* own them. It is *theirs,* and they may be protective over their stuff in a way they wish they were protected. Additionally, they could just want to protect the little that they actually have to call their own. There are countless theories and ideas that go along with foster children attaching significant worth to their stuff, but ultimately just be aware of the fact that this is a very real feeling that should be respected.

For my thirteenth birthday, my mom worked terribly hard to get *just* enough money to buy me an ipod. It was the first thing my mom had ever bought me that cost a good chunk of change, and I tried really hard to take good care of it! I recorded videos on it of my mom, mentors, and friends saying nice things about me so that when I was sad or missing them, I could just watch one of the little videos and feel better. It also had many songs that had great meaning to me, everything about this little music player made me happy and hopeful.

One day - more like multiple days, but this one day in particular - I lent my iPod to my foster sister who liked listening to the radio on it. I walked into our room to her barely keeping it together - laughing-wise. I asked what was so funny, and finally she choked out through giggles "I accidentally left your iPod on my jeans and washed them." This broke me, and she couldn't understand why. It was because something so insignificant to her - and really most people in general - had a lot of importance to me, and now it was gone. In my head, I *needed* that iPod to cope with everything, to escape for a little while. And now, I just had to stare at the ceiling and pretend that life wasn't sucking every bit of joy out of my entire being.

Overall, in telling this short story about my iPod, I would really just like you to understand that different people put importance on different things, and for you to treat one person's item as "universally" insignificant - especially that of a foster child's - could result in hurt feelings that lead to distance put between you and the child.

It's normal and quite sweet of you to want to spend quality "family" time with your foster child. In fact - it's crucial! However, it's interesting how sticky this can actually turn out to be. It is so very important to do things as a family unit, such as going out to dinner, parks, the mall, even trips to go camping or to an amusement park. You want to build these good memories and strengthen your relationship with your foster child. Though, you will encounter some bumps along the way, more often than not. Let's discuss:

- **"You're not my family"**

This is a big one - "I don't want to go on a family trip, because this isn't my family!" Says the bitter, heartbroken child. Now, personally as a foster child I wouldn't have thought too much of my foster parents saying something along the lines of "we're going to go out and do something as a family." However, that word "family" could be a very sensitive spot for some children - particularly little ones who don't understand the situation at hand, but older kids as well. So what's my point? Try to use words such as "group" instead of family for the extra sensitive children in your home, i.e. "Let's go to the park as a group and have some fun!" Or even "let's all go to the park together for some fun." Just be careful using titles such as "mom," "dad," and "family." Unless you've come to an agreement on what's appropriate to say with your foster children.

- **The child doesn't want to risk bonding with you**

This may sound a little strange, but your foster child might be scared to build a relationship with you, either because they don't want to "replace" their parents or because they're afraid of being betrayed or hurt again, so they're trying to protect themselves. Take things slow, don't rush into big family activities right off the bat. Maybe a lunch date, park time, a walk, small things first if anything at all.

- **Feeling excluded**

I remember when I was in my first foster home, we went on a trip up to a ranch. There was this one foster girl, Beverly, who included me in everything! She took me with her to go get burgers, let me stay up with her while she did homework (because I had a fear of sleeping when I was younger), and she even let me ride on the back of her dirt bike with her. It distracted me from the bad that was flooding my life and created a good memory to replace a bad one in my mind. Here's my tip - pay attention to your new foster child, pay attention to your old foster child. Overall, each child deserves to feel special and cared for as an individual rather than just grouped into "the foster kids" category. So just be mindful is all!

Compromise

A small section, but an important one. There's got to be compromise on both your part *and* the foster child's part - it's an important part of creating a comfortable environment for everyone. Not everything can go your way, and Vise Versa - not everything can go the foster child's way either. You've got to humble yourself, and your foster child has to learn the freeing quality of humility as well. Child doesn't like ice cream? Give them a cookie! Child doesn't like the park? Maybe go to the library instead, or go to the park this time and the library next time, or make an agreement. It's simple once you start getting the hang of it.

CHAPTER FIVE: SCHOOL

A for Effort

School is either easy or tough, and every kid handles school differently - every kid *learns* differently. So yes, encourage your foster children to be the best they can be! Be careful, though, because pushing them too hard can cause extra stress and anxiety that they seriously do not need, and probably can't handle. It's how hard they're working that matters the most - if they're doing their best, that's literally all they can do. Help them to always be doing their best, but don't push them so hard that they resent you and purposefully rebel and start to allow their school work to suffer.

Extracurriculars

I actually wrote an article about this for Foster Focus Magazine a couple years back. Extracurricular activities are a great way for a foster child - or any child, really - to cope with the stress, anxiety, and pain they are going through. For example, I was in show choir in high school, and being onstage entertaining the audience was so freeing and therapeutic, it gave me something to look forward to and it distracted me from my pain and heartache. Activities such as sports, theater, or even youth groups or clubs should always be discussed with your foster child. They may not want to participate in anything, but if they end up giving it a shot it could possibly be the absolute best thing for them at this time in their lives.

CHAPTER SIX: SOCIAL LIFE

The Parents

It's important to be extra careful when talking about your foster child's parents around them. I remember back in my fourth foster home, my foster sisters and foster mom were sitting around the table making fun of my mom because she wasn't able to lock her bike up correctly when coming for a visitation at one of the agencies. This may seem insignificant, or something silly to be hurt over, but I still think about it to this day and it still affects me. It's been years. When I was adopted, my adopted mom called my mother "nothing more than a pitiful drug addict," something that will always, always stick in my brain. So watch what you say about your foster children's parents - it's a very sensitive subject and nothing makes bashing mom and dad acceptable.

I hung out with a bad crowd when I was in middle school - not all of my friends were that way of course, but I thought I was cool hanging out with high schoolers that drank and smoked when I was 11 years old, and as soon as I was put in foster care none of them wanted anything to do with me. I was devastated and felt so alone and betrayed, but of course I should have known. Old friends could be a very nice thing for your foster child, but it might also be toxic - so overall, meet the friends and their parents, and use your best judgement.

New friends are also very important, your foster child doesn't need to feel more lonely than they already do. Friends provide comfort, support, and they make good memories with you that eventually x-out the bad memories, and that's so important. So never turn away the opportunity for your foster child to develop a relationship with a new friend.

Let's talk about mentors now, which are very important. I bring this up because of a terrible experience I had when I was in foster care. Amanda and Chris were my angels, the two people who took me out of a terrible situation and gave me the love and encouragement and comfort I needed whenever they could. Chris helped me with my math homework and let me play his guitar, Amanda taught me how to play the piano and make a chocolate cream pie! They are the kindest people, and I felt like, scratch that - feel like they are my family. They provided an environment and provided a relationship that gave me hope and made me feel like I was worth something. That was taken away from me, because of lies. I wasn't allowed to see or talk to them until I was adopted or else *they* would get in trouble. They had done nothing wrong to anyone, but were being punished - as was I - merely because of my foster parents' jealousy. There were other factors, such as Amanda comforting me while I was being attacked during a meeting and the social workers deeming that as inappropriate (news flash - hugging a crying child isn't inappropriate), but it ultimately boils down to my foster parents wanting to be the only adults in my life that I had a close relationship to. This is wrong and selfish. There will be teachers, youth pastors, friends' parents, neighbors, etc. that your child will start to develop a relationship with and they will look up to these people, and that is perfectly ok! You are special in a different way, but you won't be the only people that are special to them.

Every relationship is different and unique, remember that. Your child needs positive role models and positive people flooding their lives, and they can never have enough!

Ah, dating. A touchy subject for all parents. It wouldn't be appropriate for me to say "let them date!" I'm not a parent, I'm merely a former foster child who is trying to give advice from a different point of view. So here's all I have to say about dating - if you're going to allow them to date, be cautious of who they choose to date. I say this because most of the time these children are coming from homes where one parent most likely abused the other, and this is not okay. Does the child know this? Maybe, but whether or not they know, they still might not choose to stay out of the situation. Keep a watchful eye.

CHAPTER SEVEN: WHAT'S LEFT?

Labels and Expectations

I lived with a girl once who lived in a foster home whose foster parents forced her to call them mom and dad. She cried herself to sleep nearly every night. That's not right - unless you've had a conversation with your foster child where they agree they are comfortable calling you mom or dad, you should never force that upon them.

When it comes to introducing them to strangers or family members or friends, I would steer clear of referring to your foster child as your own. I remember living with someone who introduced me as her daughter, and even though it wasn't me saying it, I somehow felt like I was betraying my mom. Just be courteous and sensitive to your foster child's feelings.

Conclusion

We've covered a lot in this short book. So overall - communicate with your foster children, be sensitive towards their feelings, and give them a loving and happy home. It's really as simple as that! Remember, all I've had to say is merely advice I wanted to give because of the experiences I've had. It may not all be what you learn in your training and meetings, but it's - in my opinion - very important stuff to always keep in mind. A foster child is still a person, and they are not broken - merely bent. So what will you do to help reshape them into someone they are confident to be?